Letters I Never Wrote Conversations I Never Had

To

"Granddaddy"

Elmer Boyd Vineyard

(1884–1956)

ACKNOWLEDGMENTS

The following are a few of the people who have admonished, enlightened, and encouraged me in this endeavor as they read and responded to the letters and conversations: Dr. Bill Arnold; Rev. Milton "Bud" Fisher; C. B. "Sonny" Gill; Dr. David Hicks; Ms. Sally Hicks; Rev. Craig Loscalzo; Dr. Marion Woolard; my therapist, Dr. Abbot Schulman; and last, but most important, my wife, Lucille, and daughter, Kim.

Letters I Never Wrote Conversations I Never Had

Charles Ben Bissell

COLLIER BOOKS
MACMILLAN PUBLISHING COMPANY
New York
COLLIER MACMILLAN PUBLISHERS
London

Macmillan Publishing Company
866 Third Avenue, New York, N.Y. 10022
Collier Macmillan Canada, Inc.

Library of Congress Cataloging-in-Publication Data
Bissell, Charles Ben.
Letters I never wrote, conversations I never had.
1. Christian life—1960– . 2. Imaginary letters.
3. Imaginary conversations. 4. Bissell, Charles Ben.
I. Title.
BV4501.2.B534   1987   920′.009′04 [B]   86-21605
ISBN 0-02-016610-9

A Tilden Press Book

Macmillan books are available at special discounts for bulk purchases for sales promotions, premiums, fund-raising, or educational use. For details, contact:

Special Sales Director
Macmillan Publishing Company
866 Third Avenue
New York, N.Y. 10022

10 9 8 7 6 5 4 3 2 1

Printed in the United States of America

Contents

I
A Beginning

A BEGINNING

◆

The Letters

I never was one to write letters. It always seemed that other things were much more important. I regretted that, especially when I realized I had left a lot of things unsaid. Fortunately, with the help of my therapist, I learned it was not too late.

One afternoon I began to share with him all the people now deceased that I wanted to write but never had. Softly he said, "Why not?" Not knowing how seriously to take him, I said, "But they are dead." With genuine care he responded, "Write them anyway." How right he was. It took over six months before I could begin. Then I finally sat down and wrote my maternal grandfather, Elmer. At first the whole process felt ridiculous, and I hoped no one would ever know. Even better, I decided I would just tear it up. Then as the letter seemed to flow and new feelings surfaced, I was surprised to discover tears running down my cheeks. Years of pent-up anger and grief were finally being released from secret places in my heart. Hurt, pain, sorrow, joy, laughter, disappointment, and despair were breaking free. I felt a new surge of power and my pen could not write fast enough. Some of the words shook my soul. I had no idea they were begging, pleading, crying to be heard—no, to be felt.

After the first letter I was exhausted. Lancing a wound can leave you reeling. Yet, after a few minutes, my breathing was deep and more relaxed than I had ever experienced. It was as if an anvil had been lifted off my chest— an unnecessary burden I had carried for years.

While I was anxious to move on to a second letter, I was so emotionally drained that a week passed before I wrote again. This time it was easier. Again, I felt a little embarrassed, but then the tears came and new insight poured out. What was going on? How could something hurt and yet feel so good at the same time? More and more the words relieved pressure I was not even aware existed. I felt like the man who did not realize how his shoes hurt until he took them off. I was removing weight and loosening vises that had been the culprit of headaches and fatigue for over twenty-five years.

By the fifth letter, I was able to write two a day. Instead of feeling foolish, I could hardly wait to begin. I never knew what I would say, never preplanned a word. I simply found a quiet time, sat, and wrote whatever came to mind. It was an uncomplicated procedure, so simple that I wondered why it had taken so long to discover it. I think it also baffled me that such a simple act could have a profound effect.

One of my most helpful discoveries was that folks made me feel "big." The fact that I am 5′4″ may throw additional light on how important that was to me. Yet, I feel many who stand physically tall will have no difficulty resonating with what it means to feel *really* tall inside. Too many times I have heard, "Did I ever feel small." Like beauty, size is in the eyes of the beholder, or in the heart of the hearer.

Thus, the letters not only opened up feelings I had for others, but also how I felt when in their presence. The value of the writing grew to include much more than I imagined possible.

The Conversations

The conversations were much more difficult. Now, instead of just saying what I felt, I was faced with trying to feel how others would respond. This was perplexing enough when I thought of those I knew well. It became even more challenging when I attempted to converse with those to whom I could never remember having said a word. My Uncle Ed is the best example. I was less than three when he died. How could I know what he might say? How did he feel about me? What words would he want me to hear? I decided to attempt it anyway, and an amazing process took place. My greeting was easy enough, but then after several minutes of muddled thoughts nothing would clearly come to mind.

I began to feel foolish and started to drop the project. Then, almost out of the emptiness, I began to write. It was as if as soon as I gave up, the other person was able to speak. Words began to flow without conscious thought. I was shocked, pleased, and most often surprised by what was appearing on the paper before me.

Where did the message come from? I do not think there is any way ever to know for sure, but perhaps it is less important to know the source than to have had the experience and the growth it brought. The fact remains that I began to hear and relate to people out of my past in a new way. I began to see things not only from my perspective but also from theirs. While so much of what I said in the letters contained my pain, the conversations allowed those to whom I wrote to say how it was from their point of view.

Did I put words into their mouths? In a sense I did. However, I feel that it was more involved. For the first time I really tried to get into their shoes. Aware of the impossibility of such a task, I had felt there was no need to try. Yet, in trying, while accepting the limitations, I found the effort full of revelations and rewards beyond all expectation.

As in the letters, so in the conversations, great weights of guilt, much of it irrational, were lifted. Anger and grief, long left unexamined, surfaced and poured out like pus from a wound. Once again I began to experience cleansing. The words of the Psalmist took on new meaning:

5

Create in me a clean
heart, O God,
and renew a right
spirit within me.

This was a way to uncover old wounds that had been
covered too long. This was a way to renew my spirit as I
stopped blaming others for the pain in my life . . . pain
that I had chosen to hold; pain that punished me, not
them; pain that blotted out positive experiences and dis-
torted my memories; pain that crawled around inside my
mind corrupting the joy and leaving the sting of resent-
ments; pain that gripped my head like a vise and blinded
me to the beauty in the lives of so many who had loved
me. That was it—pain which kept me from believing I was
loved or lovable, and behind my pain I hid my true feelings. After all, they had hurt me, and when I get hurt, I
want to hurt back. Too small to do it physically, I retaliated
with my emotions. You can hurt by striking out. You can
also hurt by withdrawing. What is more cruel than withdrawal . . . refusing to give of yourself in any caring way
to another? How better to hurt than by never saying, *"I
love you," "Thank you," "You are special," "I need you,"* or *"You
make a difference"*?

The tragedy is that in hurting others I was the one who
paid the biggest price. I was the one who lost the most.

Therefore, these letters and conversations are my at-
tempts to regain some of what I had lost; give up what was
gone; and thus, learn how to say "hello" and "good-bye."

In writing these letters I also began to see a second
revelation: that often my greatest struggle was not in saying
"hello" but "good-bye." I had known for years that I found
beginnings difficult. Now, I was learning how much trou-
ble I had with endings. Never being one to give up easily,
I found myself at times too stubborn to give up at all. Yet,
I discovered that in giving up, I did not lose these significant people in my life. Instead, I gained them in a new
way. When I ceased denying their death and experienced
the grief, it became possible for me to know them as they

were. Energy I had used to cover the pain of my sorrow and anger could now be used in more productive ways. It was a joy to realize that the more I said healthy good-byes, the more I found myself able to say new hellos.

In some way my unwillingness to face my grief blocked me from encountering real joy . . . the joy of new friends and close relationships where loss is a risk, but well worth it. Only through healthy mourning and grieving can joy be restored. Thus, these letters have allowed me to say belated good-byes . . . long overdue. It has been a bitter-sweet process.

Another benefit has been to look at the reality of death. Freud was right when he said, "Our own death is unimaginable." Yet, I feel I have gently and ever so timidly come to peek at the reality of my own death. If these "heroes" and "saints" can really be dead, then so can I. The struggle to hold onto their lives is my own personal struggle to hold onto mine!

More than once I have read that real living does not begin until one faces one's own death. In a small way that happened to me in the writing of these letters. I can also attest that as scary as it has been and *is,* I have no regrets. The freedom the writing has brought is one I had never known. I feel more alive, not less. Confronting the truth that endings are a part of this life as much as beginnings opened my eyes to death and life. Beginnings and endings go together. The paradox is that to deny one and to accept the other is to lose both.

One day I will die just like all of these to whom I have written. Instead of leading me to hide, that fact calls me from my emotional cave. In thinking about death, I have discovered life and the way I spend it.

Death is inevitable, but I am not powerless. I have the ability to decide how I will use my life. The choice is mine. I can hide or come out and play. Those who know me know my decision. Ready or not, here I come!

II
Letters
I Never Wrote

Elmer

Elmer was my maternal grandfather. Standing a little less than 5′6″ with a thin, wiry frame, he was hardly the stereotypical blacksmith, but a blacksmith he was. He had marks where the horses had kicked him to prove it. Rarely seen in a tie, he was more at home in his overalls and a dirty, oil-soaked hat of which only he and I could be proud. Modern conveniences were of no interest to him. He never had running water in his home. I remember there were a few electric lights in his home and a couple of oil lamps. After all, if you go to bed when it gets dark and get up at daybreak, who needs lights?!

Though my memories are almost all positive, Elmer did have a very abrasive side. This dark side was most evident when he drank, though I knew of the problem only through family conversations. For some reason still unknown, he was never seen drinking after I was born. It was, I believe, a gift to me. However, the best gift was his unconditional love.

On August 21, 1956, he suffered chest pains. Two days later he died of a massive heart attack. He was seventy-two.

I never felt comfortable saying to him how important he was to me. This letter is an attempt to express those feelings as well as the anger which I had because of those parts of his life to which I objected.

In my office hangs a horseshoe. It is a daily reminder of a part of my heritage which I blocked for years and nearly missed completely. As I started the writing process, Elmer came to mind first.

Dear Granddaddy,

This is the first letter I have ever written you. I always had lots of things I wanted to say but somehow always held back. Maybe it was your stern, hard look that led me to believe that "strong" men did not write letters. That was something women did. Real men kept their feelings to themselves. Believing that makes me sad, for I had and have so many feelings for you.

One of the strongest feelings is a warm love. I wanted often to tell you how good you made me feel when you introduced me to your friends at the blacksmith shop. I don't remember what you said, but you surely seemed proud. You never bragged on what I had done or told folks what a "good" boy I was. It was as if you said, "He's my grandson, and that's enough to make him okay." You seemed proud and comfortable with those brief words, and they made me feel big inside. While others praised my virtues and talents, you said, "That boy is fine just like he is, and you are going to love him like I do." That was unconditional acceptance. No wonder I love you so.

One of my favorite memories is your teaching me how to whittle on a stick. I began cutting by pulling the knife toward me instead of pushing away. You laughed harder than I can ever remember. Others had laughed at me at times and it hurt. Your laughter was different. I didn't feel you were making fun of me. In fact, I remember laughing inside myself. I felt you were saying, we all make mistakes, don't worry about it, let me show you again. I love you for that.

My love for you also included angry feelings. I didn't like the way you growled at Grandmother. I loved her too, you know. You seemed so cold and insensitive to her, so much warmer and closer to me. I knew you could be caring of her and was angry when you were not. I could make lots of excuses for you, but the anger is still there. I also got angry about those years before I was born when your drinking sprees resulted in fits of violence. Those straps you used on my mother's legs led her to use straps on me and my sister. You must have been hurting inside, too. How tragic that you did not use some other way to release your anger. I hated that part of you because I knew the power and strength of the other side of you.

The fondest memory is sitting around your table for a delicious meal. You always wanted to "fatten" me up. Strangely enough, that never felt like a criticism but words of support. You were saying, "This boy deserves the best. Give him the finest and don't cut corners." I surely felt important at your table. And I liked the way you seemed to be in charge. Sometimes it scared me a little, but I admired the way you knew what you wanted. At those times you didn't seem inconsiderate, you just were clear about your own needs. Meals at your table were fun. My faith teaches me that we will have another meal together. I can just see you now telling the angels how you want a cup of coffee and a saucer. After all, you will want to drink it out of the saucer! Then you will look at me and say to the servants, "Give this boy the best you got; we still need to 'fatten' him up a little." Even in heaven you will be taking good care of me. I look forward to that special meal.

I remember the day you died. They had told me of your heart attack and how critical you were. The news that you were dead gave me a real jolt. You always were such a strong man in my eyes. Oh, I know you were short and slender. But I can still see those wiry muscles in your arms as you hammered out hot iron as if it were dough. You were for me the man of steel. How could you die! Shocked and angry, I walked the alleys. More numb than anything else, I began to deny how important you were to me. I started thinking of you as just a poor ole hard-headed blacksmith who worked himself to death. As you can see, that was my way of trying to get back at you for up and dying on me. Who was going to fatten me up with you gone? I know I had other grandparents and relatives, but you fattened up my good feelings about myself. I didn't have to do anything to impress you. I was fine even if I never fattened up. I felt your death robbed me of that, and I was furious with you. It was rage based on love and a great loss.

Your funeral still remains vividly in my mind. I hated those old men who sang. You deserved better and I wanted to say what you said about me, "He deserves the best." I can make excuses for their terrible voices because of their age but my anger boiled nonetheless. You did deserve better. I don't remember looking at you in the casket, and the graveside service I have forgotten. It was my way of denying your death. I was not ready or willing to give you up. Only this year I went back to your grave. I stood and for the first time really "knew" you were dead. I could accept it now because I knew that what you had given me not even death could steal.

Love,
Ben

Nettie

I never called my maternal grandmother one of the usual nicknames or abbreviated titles. She was simply "Grandmother," and she did all the positive things *Grandmother* conveys. She could cook delicious pies and cakes, mix up homemade biscuits without a recipe, and quilt. Best of all, she found no fault in her grandchildren, especially me.

In her early years she had picked cotton in Texas. After moving to Tennessee, she accepted her role as housewife and mother of two daughters. For the most part quiet and soft-spoken, she carried a mischievous sparkle in her eye which I always wanted to ask about but never did. I rarely heard her complain, and she usually had nothing but praise for her neighbors.

Grandmother rarely attended church, but you knew she was a believer in the best sense of the word. It was a faith I felt, though I cannot remember anything "religious" she ever did. Faith certainly can be translated without words. She proved it!

Her life seemed to revolve around her home and the small community where she lived. After a few days away, she always became uncomfortable and began listing all the reasons why she needed to get back to the home place.

After my grandfather died, she preferred to remain at home. It was her wish to care for herself as long as she could, and she did for the most part until her death at eighty-nine.

I wondered if she ever knew how significant her "quiet" manner was to me. In an attempt to let her know, I wrote the following letter.

Dear Grandmother,

The first thing I think of when writing you is that lemon pie you made each time I visited. Wow, my mouth is watering now. You never knew what a recipe was. Somehow you just started mixing everything together and before long, out came a beautiful pie heaped with meringue. As a little boy I sometimes thought you had magic . . . well, you did! And you made biscuits the same way—just mixed 'em up, threw them in the oven, and out they came, plump and tasty. Then there was the gravy. No one yet has ever made gravy like yours. Yessir, you were a magician in the kitchen. Did I ever tell you? I honestly cannot remember. I have a feeling you knew; but, oh, how I wish I had said it more. I drove by your house a few weeks ago. The feelings that bubbled up in me were so wonderful to experience. I smelled all the good food again, the flowers around the house, the apple tree, and even your dipping snuff. I again saw you sitting on the porch in the swing enjoying a spring day, seeming never to have a care. You were that way a lot. I know now that you felt more pain than you showed; yet, it seemed to take very little toll on you. I always felt calm and relaxed around you. Maybe that is why I daydream of sitting with you on the porch when I am torn apart inside. Where did the peace come from? You seldom spoke of your faith, and I don't ever remember your going to church, though you were a member. Maybe it was the songs you told me about . . . "Sweet Hour of Prayer," "What a Friend We Have in Jesus" . . . but I never heard you pray or read the Bible. Your favorite hymn was "I Am Satisfied with Jesus." Interesting. Your invisible faith was real to me. I grieve that I did not ask you more about it. My guess is you would not have known how to talk about it. You just lived it.

I think now of the kind things you did for others. I

never heard you criticize anyone, though I am sure you must have. It was as if you reached out to people as they came. You were a carer. How I felt that. Yet, at times you were fooled by others because of trusting them too much. A sad story would get you every time. Then you almost "gave away" all of Granddaddy's blacksmith tools after he died. That is my anger, not yours. You never put much stock in possessions anyway. People were important to you. I was one of those people!

Your death, though expected, was a great loss to me. I didn't realize how much you had meant to me. The funeral home was packed the evening we received friends. You surely had a lot of them. Each one was telling me how you had done special things and how much you loved me. All this just reinforced what I already felt down inside. It was an inspiring evening as we recalled some of the most pleasant memories of my life—days that will comfort me as long as I live. You surely helped a lot of people, but none more than me.

The chorus of your favorite hymn goes "I am satisfied. I am satisfied with Jesus. But the question comes to me as I think of Calvary, 'Is my master satisfied with me?' " The answer, Grandmother, is without question, "Yes, oh my, yes!"

I love you,
Ben

Ed

My dad's only full brother was killed in a plane crash in 1944 while serving in the Air Force. I was only two when he died and have no memory of ever having seen or known him. Yet, few people in my past have had such influence on me.

The family spoke often of how much we looked alike. They saw the resemblance more than I, but it was certainly there. For years I unconsciously felt a need to be like him

16

and to realize all the dreams that were Ed's. These messages, however subtle, I heard through the family. Only in the last three years have I discovered the power I had given him. In attempting to write the letter, I became aware of how little I had asked about him. On rare occasions did the family discuss anything about Ed's schooldays and what it was like growing up. What had kept us from talking of him more? What blocked me from asking? I began inquiring more after I wrote a letter that was long overdue . . . a letter to a man whom I knew only through the family stories.

Dear Ed,

I have no memory of ever having seen you. Yet, I felt your shadow every day of my life. Though you died in that plane crash, your presence lived on in me. It was not your doing; the family chose me to replace you. I guess it was because we looked so much alike. Not only did we look alike but how often I heard, "He is just like Ed." Before I realized it, I was trying more and more to be like you. I wanted to be like you. They said you were handsome, intelligent, well-liked, and loved music. You seemed to be everything the family wanted; so I chose to be you as much as they chose me to replace you.

I both loved and hated you. The love came from hearing how you loved me. Somehow I understood that you thought I was special. How I needed to believe that! I also loved you because of what you meant to my dad. It seems his heart was broken when you died. I would listen with envy and joy at the camaraderie you shared. I heard of the painful times and how much the two of you leaned on each other. I was impressed with the strength you gave each other. I loved you for caring for me, and I loved you for caring for my dad.

There was another side. I hated you for dying. You were a link to my past. You could have told me stories and shared more about what the family was like. I grieve over never having had a conversation with you. I read your last letter for clues . . . clues as to who you were and what life meant to you, clues as to why you did not live. I wondered with anger about the crash. What went wrong? Why? I was angry with those who made such planes and angry with you for flying it. I even wondered if you were careless and at fault. I needed so much to blame someone or something. I wanted an answer so badly. You see, I felt that if I had an answer it would take away my pains of grief. I know now that is not true. Reasons neither replace nor substitute for feelings. You died and I hate that fact. I miss you still.

Your death left more than a vaccum in my life. It left such a big one in the family that they chose me to fill it. Dad often jokingly introduced me as his brother. Many said we looked like brothers. Papa Bissell called me "Son." I can never remember his saying "Grandson." You were dead but you lived on in me. Unconsciously I hated you for that. No matter how hard I struggled, I sensed a need to be "Ed." It was a well-kept secret. I told no one until now. I still am not sure how I managed to bring it to my consciousness. I just know it was great to realize I could stop trying to be you. I was also able to lay down my fury and rage with you. I was so divided trying to be you and hold onto "me." I know you never meant for that to be.

Closing this letter is difficult. I find myself wanting to ask all those unanswered questions again. I look to my faith. One day, where there is no time, tears, nor death, we will catch up on all those stories you would have told. And there will be no need for me to sit in for you. There will be a place for us both. That vacuum in our family will truly be filled.

Love,
Ben

Papa

"Papa" was the name I had affectionately called my paternal grandfather. Born in North Carolina, he ran away

18

from home when he was sixteen. When I pressed to know more about the family, he would say, "It is a waste of time. They weren't much good anyway." I did not believe that but never was able to get him to say more.

Somehow I always felt Papa looked like Harry Truman. I never told him, because I got the idea he was a Republican and might not care for the comment.

He was a man who believed in a well-fitting suit and plenty of after-shave. His gait had a dignified lift that reflected power and importance.

Liked by most folks, he had a good sense of humor and when really tickled, would laugh uncontrollably. His face would turn red and tears would stream down his cheeks. Bald at an early age, he had only a little hair around each ear. His favorite story was of two flies that landed on his head. One said to the other, "When I first started visiting here, this great barren plain was only a small path." He knew how to laugh at himself.

He would challenge me to grow tall, though he stood only 5'6" himself and usually carried a few more pounds than his stature called for. I always felt he favored me but he never dared to say so out loud. When you have a good thing going, you do not trifle with it.

A churchman to the core, he taught Bible classes even when he was in his eighties. He died in 1977 after a long bout with heart problems.

Why write to Papa? I was not sure at first. I just knew there was unfinished business and hoped it would surface as I wrote. I was not disappointed.

Dear Papa,

Today I was offered several good contracts. I thought how proud you would be of me. Then, I realized I never heard a compliment from you even though I felt at times you were proud of me. I always felt you wanted me to be "great" and that you knew I could be. I longed, however, to hear your blessing. I felt it. I just never heard it. The closest you came was when you told me you wanted me to

19

have a part in your funeral. I was honored. I wonder if it was to show me off. You always liked to do that. Suddenly I realized that was the way you showed your love. How I wish you could have said it. How I wanted to hear the words that went with the feelings. Don't misunderstand, I loved the way you would strut when you told others about me. I felt tall, important, and special. It has provided lots of strength on those days when I feel so small, unimportant, and weak. Strength—that was what you gave me. I loved you for walking proud. Your clothes, cars, and house all looked so big to me as I grew up. And Christmas . . . you gave me more at Christmas, it seemed, than anyone else did. How could I help but feel special?

My anger now is that you could not say it. You were a good speaker. I often heard you pray beautiful prayers and tell God how important He was to you. I so wanted you to say those same words to me. But I never told you either. We must have had an unwritten and silent contract. We would admire one another but never speak the words. Now I wonder not so much what stopped you, as what stopped me. Was I afraid you would not praise me if I praised you? Would I discover you were just a man and the praise would somehow shatter my image of you? I grieve over never having hugged you and said, "Papa, you are a tower of strength to me. When I think of strength, I think of you." How very sad that I waited until your funeral to begin to say what encouragement you provided for my life. Only after your death did I really begin to tell others of your faith. Faith that helped you through the death of your younger son, death of a beautiful granddaughter, and the deaths of three wives. How you must have hurt; and yet, I only saw you cry once. I was shocked . . . a strong man crying. It was a great lesson. It has helped me cry.

Best of all, I remember your many visits to our house. These were Christmases, Thanksgivings, vacations, my birthdays, and graduation. The most important one, however, was the day Dad's store had burned to the ground.

I will never forget that day. I saw Dad slump that afternoon in a kitchen chair. He, too, represented strength, but this day he seemed tired and broken in a way I had never seen before. All that day he had watched as his store and years of hard work evaporated in smoke, as his inventory became ashes. No wonder he looked so completely exhausted and drained; we all felt helpless and so alone. Then we heard your car pull in our driveway. You had driven several hours from Georgia. Oh, how beautiful your face looked to me that day. You came in the kitchen and, like Job's friends, you sat with us in our misery. Unlike Job's friends you offered no simplistic answers. That was one day you didn't need to speak. Just being there did it all. It seems that within a few hours Dad was actually laughing again. When I heard the two of you laugh, hope sprang again in my soul, and I knew we would make it. Oh, how I loved your laughter. That day it was better than fire insurance. It was medicine for our broken hearts. Now when my dreams seem to go up in smoke, I recall *that* day, hear you and Dad laugh, and say, "I can make it . . . strength . . . strength will come. 'I will mount up with wings of eagles, I will run and not be weary. I will walk and faint not.' "

Thanks, Papa, Thanks for strength. I am so proud of you!

Love,
Ben

Mama B

Everyone's voice is unique. That was especially true of Mama B. While you may think of most grandmothers' voices as soft, hers carried a tone that would lead you to believe that she was always hoarse, just getting over a cold. At times that voice would frighten me a little but the fear was based on anything but fact.

She always seemed taller, though she stood only 5'8". I

21

can still see her wire-rimmed glasses and gray hair reflecting the sun on those summer days in Georgia. She had a warmth that often seemed just under the surface and would break through at unexpected but appropriate times. In fact, she had a way of coming through just when things would seem to be futile. Her ability to reach out to me still holds me up, even now.

I doubt anyone ever cared more and wanted more for me. Actually, she was my step-grandmother. I never knew my dad's mother. Mama B and her two sons had joined ranks with Papa B and his two sons to form the family as I knew it. She was a good choice. I never told her, but this belated letter tries. Her death in 1952 came after a long struggle with leukemia.

Dear Mama B,

Once I heard someone say that folks who die are still able to see what goes on with their relatives. I always believed you knew about me and watched my every move with loving eyes. I didn't feel that way about other people who died, but I sensed your presence almost all the time. When I would do something well or receive an award, inside a voice would say, "Mama knows." I find that strange because I was often afraid of you. It was not that you ever touched me in anger or said any unkind words. I believe it was your stern manner and raspy voice. Whatever you said to do, I did almost before you were through asking. I doubt you ever realized how powerful a woman you seemed to me. It made it impossible for me to hug you until you were in the hospital dying of leukemia. How I love and hate that day. Hate it because you were dying; love it because you wanted me to hold you . . . hug you . . . and you even kissed me. I never saw you alive again, but that day changed how I would remember you—not as strong, stern, and unfeeling, but as soft, tender, and loving. I hated that day because it revealed what could

22

have happened many times before. I loved that day, for-without it I would have missed a beauty you never shared before. No wonder I believed you watched over me. Who wouldn't want such caring arms around them day and night?

Your funeral was beautiful. That may seem like a strange word. I can see the church filled with people and flowers. It was a service for a queen. I was so glad to be a part of those who said good-bye. I did not cry. I didn't feel you would want me to. I wanted to be strong for you like you had been for me. I have cried since . . . tears of anger over loss of your physical presence (see, I still feel you near) and tears of joy over the last hug that meant more than all the other times put together. More and more I discover how very little I knew about you. I don't recall any advice you ever gave, any songs you ever sang, or stories you ever told. Surely you must have done these things, but my memory holds only your calculated, organized movement in your home. Everything seemed planned and in order. No wonder I have such a proclivity for organizing every-thing—you were a model. That kind of style surely did pay off at Christmas. Your home had so many decorations, neatly and attractively displayed. Your home was a show-place. I especially remember the glass coffee table that you transformed into an ice-skating rink. I can still see the skaters in their winter coats and red faces. They seemed so happy. You could bring happiness to others and often did. Like so many of our family, you were better at giving than receiving. Again, I better understand why I am so much the same way. I am more like you than I realized.

As I close, I long to repeat that last hug. That cannot be and I know it. However, I do thank God for that spirit of yours that surrounds me even as your arms did on *that* day. Until I see you, that will hold me . . . hold me . . . What an appropriate choice of words.

I love you,
Ben

Dave

I knew Dave for less than one year. He lived down the hall from me in college. If I was the most scared freshman, he was the most brazen. He seemed neither to fear nor worry about anything. He still holds the record for most-cuts-in-the-chapel-and-still-remaining-in-school. Few students could compete with his ability to fall asleep in class. He was brilliant but often managed to be his own worst enemy. Rules and regulations never seemed to affect him, though I never knew of his ever breaking one that hurt anybody but himself. I also never knew anyone who did not like Dave, and that included the professors who stayed perplexed as to what to do with him. He was fun and created fun wherever he went.

I am still not sure what drew us together. He was small like myself and that was part of it. However, he had a zest for life I craved. I guess I was always wanting to catch it. I learned he had been a "miracle" baby who doctors thought would die almost after birth. His recovery made news in a national magazine. He still carried the asthma that threatened him in those first weeks of life and finally claimed him at only nineteen. After Dave had left for summer vacation, he was enjoying a special weekend when the attack struck. He left behind a poem describing death but memories that speak of life.

This letter is my attempt to say a "good-bye" that was long overdue.

Dear Dave,

I looked for you that second year at school even though I knew you would not be around. It was easy to act as if you were just away on one of your visits back home or at a friend's. I am surprised how little I spoke of you at first and then rambled on to everybody about our good times.

I am positive I have related a thousand times that experience when we made our fateful trip to Morristown. With no car and almost no money, we hitched a ride for a big Friday night on the town on that pleasant spring evening. How well I remember that by 7:30 we had spent all our money and had no place to go. Then we got the idea of going to the drive-in and finding one of our buddies there who had a car. Boy, the look on the manager's face when we asked if we could go in and find our friend so that we could borrow a few dollars. He must have laughed all over inside and outside. He is probably still telling that one. Well, you decided to go around back and climb over the wall and get the money. After an hour I really was worried. Then you appeared with dirt all over your clothes, and shoes looking like two deformed mud pies. Out of breath, you told of how you had climbed over but could not find our buddy. Then I laughed until I cried as you described getting back out of the lot. My favorite line is that of a patron who saw you making your exit and said, "I've seen them climb in but I ain't never seen them climb out." Your death could never rob me of those moments. They are more valuable than the diploma. It is only paper to be read and displayed. Those moments are felt and replayed.

I envied your ability to write beautiful essays and poetry. You could do it and never use a single punctuation mark. You felt others more capable of doing that. Your gift was to create the words. As you would say, "Hey, man, that's your problem. You choose the punctuation. I just provide the words." I loved that! Freedom. I never met a man more free. You seemed to know better than all of us that life is not forever, living is for now. What an example you gave us. The sad part is that most of us are afraid to follow it.

I cried that summer day when I read you had died. My tears were of pain and anger mixed: pain at my loss and anger that it all seemed so unfair. After finding a friend who loved me closer than a brother, he was gone without warning or even time to say good-bye. I hated that part, but as usual I busied myself in order not to think. The pain was too much. I don't give up easily, and I sure as hell was not letting you go so easily.

Time has changed a lot of things but not my love for

25

you. I often thought we were like Jonathan and David. I would have risked my life for you and would now if I could.

Memorial services were held, and I heard lots of words, but I never believed they were able to describe your indomitable spirit. That spirit has made it difficult for me to accept your death and say good-bye.

I often tell folks that no one is like anyone else. You were even more so! Thanks, Dave. I love you.

Good-bye,
Ben

James

On my wife's thirty-eighth birthday her brother died while in surgery. He was thirty-three. The death was a deep blow because it was so unexpected. He left behind a wife and two children, ages five and one. Tall, dark, and handsome fit "Jim." He dressed sharply and was meticulous about his personal appearance. What was going on inside him was never quite as evident. He rarely shared his feelings even though he was sensitive to the feelings of others.

He was industrious, possessed good business savvy, and had a genuine interest in others. Those qualities paved the way for his success in the insurance business. Willing to give of his time to the church or community, he often received recognition for his civic endeavors. Many a child went to camp or received help because of his anonymous financial assistance. The hospitals looked forward to his visits when he would dress as a clown and cheer the children.

His quiet nature was often deceiving, for he did enjoy telling stories and entertaining when he could choose the time and occasion. I guess few people were ever privileged to know the many facets of his life. His dying at such a young age reduced that possibility a hundredfold.

Of all the letters, none was more difficult. No wonder, for I had denied so much grief and anger. It took this letter to break the walls that held it all in. Few deaths make any sense; his certainly did not.

Dear James,

My first struggle was whether to begin by calling you Jim or James. I realize I chose the more formal because I never got to know very well the "Jim" that was hidden inside you. On occasions "Jim" appeared with the warm broad smile and humorous anecdotes. Most of the time, however, I only knew "James," a quiet, distant, and emotionally removed young man. My grief now is that I colluded with you in allowing you to hide. At times I guess I feared the rage I sensed inside your often tender and sensitive soul. I didn't know what the anger was all about, and I was too afraid to ask. Anger was never a friend of mine when I knew you. That makes me sad because we both lost so much, and now I long for days with you that cannot be.

The first time we met is not a part of my conscious memory. My first impressions are of your tall stature, good looks, and reserved manner. You always seemed to know what you wanted and you went after it. Your voracious appetite is also a memory that remains vividly with me. I recall once your consuming enough chili at our home to feed two families. My feeling is that the real hunger was deeper. Somehow I sensed you wanted us to touch you more and speak less. I get angry thinking how we let you hide behind that strong front. You covered a tender heart in seemingly impenetrable concrete. God, how I hate you for that. The tenderness was there. I saw it on rare occasions, but even then you tried to hide it. You would dress in your clown outfit and go entertain children and do it for free. A beautiful deed, a caring, meaningful act, but you hid behind the costume. I often wonder if hide-and-

27

seek was not your favorite game. Oh, how I hurt because we did not look for "Jim" more often. You hid too well. You were too good at the game and, therefore, we never really found you.

No one could hide like you. The weekend the girl you wanted to marry said "no," you spent with us. That "no" would have left me in tears. More than a few young men have taken their lives over such rejection. You—well, you hid behind that steel door. I could not believe how little you said . . . how you went on as if nothing had happened. I did want to grieve with you. My heart ached, and you hid. I know you had a right to hide—we all do—but I hated the hiding, for it robbed me of you. I realize I am hypocritical. I am a hider, too. It is scary to let people "find" you. Oh, God, help us to come out of hiding.

I wouldn't be honest unless I also said I am angry at your dying on Lucille's birthday. As foolish as it sounds, I often felt you did it on purpose. Were you afraid we would forget you? Were you afraid of hiding and being lost from us forever? I love you, but feel the love is undeveloped because I got to know so little of you. Anger, grief, love—they all swirl around in my body until I cannot sort them out. Oh, "Jim," I do love you and will come looking for you in that "day" when no one either can or will need to hide.

Ben

Eb

Upon arriving at my first pastorate after seminary, I was introduced to Deacon Eb. Standing over six feet and having a large frame, he was an impressive figure. Already retired, he offered his time to make my beginning a positive one.

At first I was suspicious. Rumors had it he had a temper and on occasion would be ready to fight. I already knew how some deacons could start out gentle and then almost overnight be transformed into bears. To be told I had one who was always ready for a tussle left me wondering if I should not have considered the job a bit longer. My fears, however, were groundless, and in a few weeks we were close friends. It was only six months later that he died of a massive heart attack. Those were six months that produced a friendship more meaningful than some of six years. Eb could not do enough. He spoke of the struggles of the church and his own life. Folks noted that instead of being grouchy and intimidating he had a new gentleness and zeal in working with others. No pastor could have asked for a better introduction to a new field of service. His sudden death was even more of a jolt when I found myself responsible for conducting the funeral services of one who had been my mentor. He probably never realized how much he did in such a brief time. This letter is my tribute to him.

Dear Eb,

More than a dozen years have passed since we first met, and yet I can still vividly remember the first time I saw your tall frame. You looked both impressive and a little scary to me. I was just out of seminary and taking on my first full-time church. I had enough fears and goals to fill a book the size of an unabridged dictionary. What I needed was someone to calm my fears and temper my goals. You were the man.

Beginnings have always been difficult for me, and this time was no exception. You seemed to sense that. Without pushing, you would call and offer to introduce me to members of the church and community. More than once you tactfully suggested we make a hospital call or cautioned me as to who was related to whom—a critical factor in almost any church.

Rumors had come to me that you had a temper, and I should be careful around you. It was no secret that you had raised some sand in the church on more than one occasion. I found you caring, and never knew the other side they described.

I felt I had known you for years after only a few weeks. Therefore, when you died just six months after my arrival, it was a stunning blow. I can still hear the phone ringing in the early hours of the morning. A lady's voice is saying you have died. Still half asleep, feeling it was a dream, I made some unintelligent comments, and the lady explained it all to me again. She repeated your name and said you had a heart attack and died. More from instinct than conscious thinking, I said that I would be right over. As I sat with your wife, the house seemed more empty than I can describe. I had sat on that same couch with you and never noticed the size of the room. That night it seemed larger than the house itself. It was my first realization that your death left a big void in my life.

Ironically, another member of the church died that same morning. Your funeral and his were held the same day. I guess the pressure of the two funerals has blocked much of my grief until now. There seemed to be no time to allow myself to mourn your loss, for I had to turn immediately and comfort another family. Maybe that was my way of denial. I have learned by now how deceptive I can be, not so much with others as with myself.

You were a big man, Eb, not only physically, but you were big in caring, loving, and sharing yourself. Somehow I keep seeing those big brown shoes you wore. They looked huge to me and they were. It feels as if you used those shoes to make footprints for me to follow those first six months. You cut a wide path through the wilderness for me until I could find my way. I believe you must have heard, "Well done, thou good and faithful servant."

That is why I write you after all these years. I miss you. I love you. I appreciate all those thoughtful acts, words, and gifts. You genuinely cared for me. Thanks for making a trail.

God bless you,
Ben

Hazel

Bubbly, brash, and as subtle as a Mack truck—that was my Aunt Hazel. If you were looking for pretense, you would be most disappointed. She was who she was. She was my mother's sister, but it was hard at times to believe they were related. Hazel often said to my mom, "I'll stay in the kitchen and cook the meal; you do all the proper entertaining of the guests." I doubt if she realized how well she could entertain. There were few if any piano players in the state who equaled her enthusiasm while playing ragtime music. It was a delight to watch her perform. That was one time she felt no need to stay in the kitchen. Later in life she played for the Methodist Church—after toning it down some, of course.

For years she worked as a nurse in the local hospital. Add to this the fact that she lived in the same area for more than three-fourths of her life, and you can understand why it was impossible to find anyone who did not know her.

Grief was certainly no stranger to her. The death of her son, Dwight, at twenty-three, left a deep scar. Her father died two years later in the same month, and a few years later her husband. Her daughter's husband died in an explosion; and if that were not enough, she went through burying her granddaughter. More than once I wondered how she recovered from such blows.

To say she was courageous is an understatement. When told she would lose her legs due to diabetes, she refused the operation. No complications developed, and it was never discussed again. It was her heart that ended her life. Like her father, she had a fatal attack in March 1981, at the age of sixty-eight.

I had written Hazel before. This was an attempt to fill in many of the feelings I had not had the courage to express.

Dear Aunt Hazel,

This is not the first letter I ever wrote you, but I realize it is only the second. What hurts so badly is how you valued

31

that first letter. Mom told me you saved it and treasured all the things I had said. According to her, it gave you a real boost those last months before your death. I wish I could remember what I said, but I cannot. Knowing it meant so much is bittersweet: the pain over only one letter; the joy over all that it meant.

I wonder if I told you how I enjoyed those summers at your home. They are still special to me. I can see your coffee cup and smell that special aroma. You gave me my first cup of coffee, with lots of cream and sugar, of course. I felt like a big man at your table that morning. Even today, holding a cup of coffee gives me a sense of being bigger and more powerful. Maybe a better word is accepted. That surely is what I felt that *"coffee"* morning.

At times you could also make me feel smaller. I hated it when you introduced me as your sweet little nephew. The emphasis always seemed to be on the word "little." That was a sore spot for me. Then when I became a minister, you would say, "He is the little minister in our family." Oh, how I wanted to scream, "Please leave off the 'little.' " Even with the passing of years, I still get knots in my stomach and hair raises on my neck when I hear that "little" introduction. It really turned me inside-out, because on one level it felt like a boast and on another like a put-down. While I evaluated and churned, the topic of conversation went elsewhere. Maybe I should have asked for a cup of coffee!

Then there was the old player piano. Shucks, you didn't need the rolls. You could play it better without them. I can close my eyes and see you pounding and rattling that old piano with ragtime music that no roll could ever produce. That happy side of you with the deep laugh provided a resource of pleasant memories that will never be exhausted. Like good old movies, I replay those days in my mind on many occasions when the blues start to slip up on me.

Not until your death did I face the many sorrows you had experienced. One by one I recalled Dwight's death,

Granddaddy's death, Uncle Lon's death, Grandmother's death—a son, a father, a husband, a mother—then a granddaughter and great-granddaughter. How could we be surprised it was your heart that killed you? It had been broken. Your strength through all the tragedies always amazed me. A part of me wants to be strong like you; another side wants to reach out more to others for help. Maybe you were too "strong." I have often paid greatly for carrying so much all alone, but for you it was familiar, even destructive. I am not criticizing, just wishing you had felt free to share more of yourself. Then, who knows, maybe you would be here now with more to give and more to receive.

My final thoughts center on how you felt that I would always do well. I can't remember your ever saying those words, but deep down I got that feeling. What was it you did? How I would love to know. Nevertheless, it is another firm stone upon which I stand when I get that sinking feeling. I just tell myself, "Aunt Hazel believes in you; you can do it." I never said thanks for that gift. I do so now. God bless you.

Love,
Ben

Dwight

Nearly everyone has a favorite cousin. Dwight was mine. My mother's sister's first son, he was eleven years older than I. The age difference never seemed to bother him. I am amazed to this day how available he was when I wanted to play or go somewhere special. I am sure he was not always around, but he surely seemed to be. His broad smile carried an acceptance that words could never convey.

To see "The Fonz" was to see Dwight. Good-looking, cool, and chased by the girls, he could play the role without a single rehearsal. He would not need to watch the show;

33

he lived it. Often I watched him work on cars, amazed at how he could make his car engine roar. I did not realize at the time that his car needed a muffler!

The times I spent with him were mainly in the summer when we would visit my aunt. The trips were few, but the impact was great. He, without a doubt, was my hero. He was taking a friend home when his motorcycle went out of control on gravel and caused his death at the young age of twenty-three. That day left me reeling. I did not know how much he meant until I wrote this letter. It is not easy to give up one's "hero."

Dear Dwight,

I miss you more often than I am willing to admit. You provided so many good times for me. I always felt you really liked me and went out of your way to see that I had a good time. Do you remember the times you played baseball with me? I don't think you even liked the sport much, but for my sake you were willing to play. You were more of a hero to me than you ever knew. I always felt safe around you. Maybe that is why I also thought it was you who saved me from drowning at the lake that day. I surely do remember feeling that I was gone and then those strong hands came under me and pulled me to shore. I found out years later it was your daddy and not you who did it. I guess I remembered it that way because you had "saved" me so many times before. You took up for me. I never was afraid when you were around.

You really were strong. I like to recall the stories you would tell about how much more you could do on the loading docks than the other guys. Only in recent years did I realize that you were not much taller than I. You surely seemed much bigger.

I also hear your warm laughter. You always laughed *with* me and never *at* me. I seemed to please you whatever I did. Such acceptance has been rare for me. That is why your death was difficult for me to accept.

I was playing outside when the call came. My mother came out screaming to our neighbor that you had been killed in a wreck. I could not even understand what was going on. I didn't cry, but my heart felt like someone had torn a piece out of it. I was stunned.

The family chose not to let me attend the funeral. I think I hate that most of all. On the other hand, it let me deny that you really died. Inside I was angry because I felt you had abandoned me. I was small and weak. You were big and strong. I had lost someone else that would be my friend through life. The hurt is still here. I want so much to believe you are alive. I want to visit your house and entertain your children as you did for me. I am so furious that you took so many risks. Now, I know your outward strength must have covered the feelings you held inside. There was warmth and care in your touch. Somehow it seems we did not touch back. I hate that part. I have done it so often with so many. I hope your memory and your loss will help me touch more and write fewer painful letters like this.

I could not close without saying how proud I felt the day I rode in your stock car. It was noisy and scratched, but I felt like a king riding around the track with you before the race. It helps me remember that I always felt important when I was with you. I feel you loved me very much. I surely loved you. How I wish I had said it! Be sure that your care for me is not lost. I will always remember what it felt like and try to share it with other "little" boys and girls.

This letter has been difficult to close. It seems something is missing . . . something unsaid. No, it is just that once again I don't want to say good-bye. I didn't before and I don't now. Oh, I know you are dead, but I don't have to like it. Maybe it is unhealthy denial, but right now all I can say in closing is, "See you later."

Love,
Ben

Sandy

A beautiful young lady—these are the words that first come
to mind when I recall my cousin Sandy. She had inherited
the best of both parents in looks. Though only one year
older than I, I often felt she was more. She seemed to
know so much about life.

I can hear her voice speaking in soft, sensuous tones or
breaking into fiery tirades. She did have a temper that
could be triggered at the most unexpected moment. Then,
there was her laugh. I loved it. It was infectious. I felt close
to her when she would respond to something she felt was
funny. Rarely did I ever have to guess where she was emotionally.

In 1965, at the age of twenty-six, she died from a fire
in her home. She was married and the mother of two
children; her death rocked the family. Deaths are not easy
to accept and this one certainly was no exception. She was
gone, but not those early years when we played together
as children. The following letter is my attempt to deal with
my own guilt, anger, and grief over having failed to attend
her funeral.

Dear Sandy,

I find myself still trying to understand why I did not
attend your funeral. The excuse I used was being in grad-
uate school and too far away. Neither of these seems to be
the real reason. Deep inside I believe it was my unwillingness to accept your death. You were so young; so was I.
If it could happen to you, it could happen to me. I have
long regretted now not making the trip for your service.
Often I think of the irony of my studying at the seminary
so that I might offer care in times of death, and I was
unable or unwilling even to experience the grief in my
heart. It was a big mistake . . . one I have not repeated
since. Forgive me.

I guess the biggest fear was the fact that you had died

in a fire. Fire has scared me ever since that day I was burned at a bonfire by a piece of flying cardboard. Even as I write I remember the panic that went through me. It turned out to be less than severe, but the scar from the fear went deep. I also was angry with you because it sounded like you had been careless. Inside I screamed, "How could you? You know better. Don't do this to us. I love you and miss you. How could you?"

After all these years the hurt is still there. I am amazed that I have been able to lock it up so long. What a heavy load it has been. Every day somewhere in my mind your death was stored away in an attempt to deny it really ever happened. I cannot do that anymore. I am tired of lying to myself. It serves no purpose. As I find myself breaking free from the irrational guilt and fear, I am beginning to remember all the good times that I had locked up with the pain.

I can still see us sliding down a snowbank in Kentucky on garbage can lids, playing in a stream in Tennessee, laughing and acting foolish at Papa's house in Georgia. Those sweet memories burst within me now that I am able to look. I see your beautiful face. You were a gorgeous woman. I doubt you ever realized the beauty you possessed.

Then there was also your temper. My, no one could throw a temper tantrum like you! At times I thought you and the world were coming apart. The reason it bothered me was because I was sitting on a ton of rage myself. More than once you acted out my anger for me. How I wanted to rant, scream, and kick. Those fears that held me back did not inhibit you. Secretly I was saying, "Way to go, Sandy . . . Wish I could do that."

Strong-willed was the word often used about you. It was as if you always knew what you wanted and expected, if not demanded, it. I liked that, too. I often just stood and took what was dished out and thought, "Sure wish I was strong-willed like Sandy." You may remember that I never confronted you. No way. You were sure, and questions were out of the question!

The sorrow I feel today is that you never got to know the stronger side of me. It has taken decades to surface and somehow I find myself wanting you to know. I want to hear you say, "Ben, I knew you had it in you. Glad you scream and holler a little like I did."

How do I say good-bye to you? I cannot change the fact that I missed your funeral. That is my loss, not yours. However, I can begin anew to allow more of the pain and joy of our relationship to break forth. I will stop denying your death and begin remembering your life. It is a well of precious memories from which I shall draw every day remembering that we will meet again where no fears can ever keep us apart.

I love you,
Ben

Lori

My first funeral for a child was in May 1970. Today, after twenty-one years of standing beside families, none has affected me as this one. Lori was only five years old, a vibrant little girl who had a severe diabetic condition. She required two shots a day and lots of medical attention by the physician. To see her you would never know. She played and sang like all the other children.

In every congregation there is one child who, for some unknown reason, gets your attention. It was a beauty that could neither be described nor captured on canvas. It was a beauty that could only be felt.

In the three years that I knew Lori, I learned a great deal about her from her grandfather. Realizing how difficult it is for grandparents to be objective, I still found myself inspired by Lori's enthusiasm for life. She was a joy whose death raises questions to which this life does not give answers.

The letter not only allowed me to express my care and

love for Lori, but also my anger toward God. I sent Him a carbon copy.

Dear Lori,

Today I saw a lovely girl with beautiful eyes just like yours. It brought back memories of those Sunday mornings you would sit at my feet and listen to the children's sermon. Your bright, wide-awake, sparkling eyes made me feel I was the best storyteller who ever lived. Each week I would look out over the congregation to see if you were present, and usually you were. It is interesting that I recall your never saying more than a few brief words. You didn't need to, for your eyes said it all.

Every now and then I look for you as I did on those Sundays. As today when I see a delightful teenager or a five- or six-year-old little girl, then your face comes to my mind. I realize how important you were to me and that your death was more of a loss than I have been willing to admit.

The night you died I left the hospital still in shock. It didn't really hit me until I walked into my own daughter's room and saw her safely sleeping in her crib. Suddenly, the tears began to flow down my cheeks, and I wept with deep uncontrollable heaves. My wife and I held one another and I knew what we were both thinking. It could have been our child. That single thought made your death almost more than either of us wanted to face. Our tears were over the pain we guessed your parents must have felt. They were also tears over the fragile nature of life and how quickly it can be lost. Your death awakened us to the preciousness of each moment. It was a lesson we felt had come at too high a price.

It seemed so unfair. You were so young, so beautiful, so sharp . . . Why? It was so insane. I was furious with God. How could He allow this? I had held funerals for many older people, but never for a child like you. I was so hurt, angry, and stunned that I was not sure I could even do it. What could I say about such a senseless death? I had always been able to look at things logically. Your death robbed me of all my logic and caused me to look deeper into my faith than ever before. There really was no explanation, and I hated that. I wanted an answer. I searched the scriptures frantically those two days to make it come out in reasonable fashion. It was a futile attempt. Then at the funeral home your mother made a statement that broke my heart. She looked me in the eye and softly but firmly said, "The first question I am going to ask when I get to heaven is 'Why?' " Suddenly, I realized behind her anger and grief there was faith . . . no answer, just raw faith that said, "I believe I will see God. I believe I will get to ask and there will be an answer." That was the balm I needed on my aching wound.

I do not recall everything that I said that day, but I did share your mother's quote, one much like David used on the death of his child. "He cannot come to me, but I can go to him."

There was also comfort from one of your best friends, Steve, who at the age of four had great insight. He was confused by our tears and asked why we were crying. When he was told because you were in heaven, his simple, childlike response was, "Then, why *are* you crying?" There it was again. No answer, just faith. *Just* faith!

Today I make my living basically talking and writing. I use words, thousands of them over and over. Yet, now I realize that you were the vibrant little girl that taught me how much more can be said with just your eyes. I treasure that gift from you and all the other memories you provided that help me stay excited about life.

Thank you, Lori, and in faith I believe one day I will be able to look into those eyes, tell you another marvelous story, and say, "I love you."

Your pastor,
Ben

III
Conversations
I Never Had

A Conversation
with Elmer

"Hello, Granddaddy"

It was a warm spring day, and at last the ground was starting to thaw. It was a perfect day for talking . . . a perfect day to visit Granddaddy Elmer's blacksmith shop and have that long overdue conversation. I could hear his hammer slamming against metal. The old barn he had converted into a shop did not look like much without paint and with a scattering of holes in the walls. There were no lights, just the sun and the glow of the fire which softened the metal. It surely was not much to look at, but the way he walked around you would have thought it was a castle.

The door was open—always was—even when it rained, needed the light, you know. "Hello, Granddaddy. How you doing?"

Without looking up from his work, he called back, "Come on in . . . workin' on a shoe." He then grabbed a pair of tongs and lifted a red-hot horseshoe from the coals and hammered some more. His small arms swung with purpose as the steel began to take shape.

"Boy, Granddaddy, you really are working that horseshoe over. You surely have mastered the art."

A puzzled look crossed his face. "Art? Ain't no art. Art is what you been takin' in them special schools. Shucks, this is jest plain hard work. Folks get prizes for art. Never got no prize for this job. Shore do get some real gripes if you don't make it right."

Now, I was puzzled and asked, "You mean you don't enjoy it?"

With a long look that only patient grandparents have, he replied, "You shore do choose funny words, boy. First you talk about 'art' and now 'enjoy.' Son, this is hard work—

man's work. This ain't no picnic. You don't enjoy work, you jest do it."

After a little thought I offered that possibly sometimes the two go together. He didn't think so and said firmly, "They never have for me. At least I never thought of it that way. My job is puttin' food on the table, takin' care of my family, and payin' what I owe." He paused, looked out one of the holes in the wall and thought out loud, "Don't believe any of my friends ever said they enjoy their work either. Like me, they just do it."

Not willing to let it drop there, I prodded, "I always felt you had pride in your work."

"Pride?" he said laughing. "Another one of them words. You always were full of words—a real talker. No wonder you make your livin' that way. But you said a good one this time 'cause I do have pride. Only thing is I don't see how enjoyin' and havin' pride go together. A man owes it to his customers to do good work. Ain't no need to do it if it ain't worth havin' or if it don't work. That's the problem today. Too many things just ain't worth havin' and even if they were, half the time they don't work. Fact of the matter, lots of people don't work anymore. (He gives one of his rare laughs and follows it with a mischievous grin.) Can't trust people either, especially banks."

"Not even an honest one?"

"Don't believe such a creature exists. I tried bankin' in the thirties. Lost nearly every dime I had. Swore right then I'd take care of my own money." The tightness in his jaws and squinting eyes revealed only a small part of the pain and anger he must have felt surfacing. I tried a lighter note.

"Is that why you always sleep with your trousers under your pillow?"

"Darn right. That way a man knows exactly where his money is. Hard as thunder to steal a man's wallet when he's sleepin' on it."

I laughed and decided it was time to go down another track. "What do you do for fun?"

44

"Well, sure do love my coffee. Now, there just ain't anything much better in life than a good mornin' cup of coffee."

"That's all? What about games, parties, vacations?"

For the first time he seemed a little disgusted, but recovered and went on. "Ben, that stuff is for the rich. When it's daylight I get up and go to work. When it's dark, I go to bed. Not much time in between for anything else."

That sounded final to me, and I had one big question to ask. My heart pounded and stomach turned as I mounted courage to say, "You used to drink."

It was as if I had hit him so hard that he could not get his breath. Then quietly he breathed, "I am sorry to say I did. That surely wasn't no fun. Sad part is I could get real mean. I didn't want to hurt nobody. I just wasn't myself."

I wanted to rescue him from the pain and broke in, "They say you never drank again after I was born."

"Yep, that's true. Figured I had already done enough harm. No need to repeat foolish mistakes. A man sometimes gets real blind to his ways. Somehow when you came along I sort of woke up. It wasn't easy to stop drinkin' at all, but I felt it was necessary. I guess the real reason was I feared your mama would never let me see you if I kept up the drinkin'. I did want you to be able to visit me."

My heart was pounding again but this time it was not fear but joy—a wonderful feeling of being wanted. The moment also allowed me to tell him what I had held back too long already. "I wanted to see you, too. I loved to come and visit, especially in the summers. I used to wonder if you looked forward to it as much as I did."

"Figures you were wonderin' about that. Lord knows it was fun to have you 'round. Takin' you to work, though, scared me a little 'cause you were always gettin' into things and findin' some way to get extra dirty. Your mama said, 'Don't let him get hurt or dirty.' I believed to her gettin' hurt and dirty were one and the same. I was proud to show you off. Not sure why." He laughed again. "You never were good at the things I tried to teach you. Nearly cut your finger off when I tried to show you how to whittle.

Talkin' was your thing, and they laughed at how you would jabber on. You knew lots of words but shy or quiet were never two of them." Again a rare, hearty laugh.

Now, I realized I had come to the real moment of truth. I wanted more than anything else a hug. Could he do it? Could I ask? I took a deep breath and blurted, "I love you, Granddaddy . . . sure would like a hug."

Caught off guard, he sounded like an echo. "A hug?" Then rebounded with a stern, "We're men. The only men I ever saw hug was Russians and I sure ain't no Russian." He looked at me, saw the tears, took a deep breath of his own and cursed, "Well, hell, you ain't no Russian." Then he embraced me as he had done when I was child. For a moment I thought I saw a tear in his eyes. Even if it was, he would never admit it.

When I finally could speak, all I could say was, "Thanks, Granddaddy. I needed that."

Without another word I waved good-bye and knew we had had our first real conversation. I sadly walked away because I had waited so long. Yet, happy because the day had finally come . . . better satisfied until the day we will speak not through a letter or book but face to face. Then, on that day, I will not ask for permission. I will just hug him!

A Conversation with Ed

"Welcome Home, Ed"

One summer day after a lunch consisting of a bologna sandwich and an R.C. Cola, I retreated to my favorite tree. It grew beside a small stream that raged in the rains of March and April and returned to a trickle by the end of June. That was where I relaxed and dreamed . . . dreamed of things to be and of things that never could be. It was there that I saw Ed, and we had our first conversation. He was sharply dressed in his uniform, safely back from the war. He had asked where I was and was directed to my special place. I heard his steps and turned. What a terrific surprise! I jumped up and ran to him, and we shared a big "Welcome home" hug. In fact, my first words were, "Welcome home. Welcome home, Ed."

He gave a big smile and said, "Boy, have I looked forward to seeing you. We sure have a lot of catching up to do. His words carried an invitation I had waited years to hear.

I quickly replied, "I feel the same way, but I don't seem to know where to start. After years of anticipating this moment, I am going blank. Too excited, I guess."

"It is hard to talk to your double." (He knew. He knew how I felt.)

Quieter now, I mumbled, "Maybe that's it. It is almost like trying to talk to myself. Do you realize how much alike the family sees us? At times I felt I was lost in you, and if you did return, they would not need me anymore. Sounds kind of crazy, but that is what I felt."

My words obviously had touched him. "That was a heavy load. But you and I are not the same, even if the family sees us that way."

With a questioning look I eagerly asked, "How are we different?"

"You are outgoing, talkative, and right in the middle of what's going on. As one fellow said of you, 'You are a party looking for a place to happen.' " (I liked that.) "But me . . . I have always been quieter, not shy but quieter than you. I waited for others to take the first step and speak the first word. You plan the party, and I will come. Don't expect me to entertain like you or tell funny stories. I am a better listener."

"That surprises me. Somehow I never thought of you as that quiet." Anxious to hear more I asked, "Are there other differences?"

"Take music. We both enjoy listening to it. But you play an instrument and write music. I never did either. I listen; you play. You see, you have heard so many times how much we look alike that you began to believe we thought

47

and felt alike. No wonder you were scared. Angry, too, I bet."

He hit a sore spot, but I couldn't deny it. "I sure was. I felt like a copy instead of an original."

"Oh, you're an original. So am I. I don't want you to try and replace me anymore than you want to. How do you think I feel when people talk like you have replaced me? I want to be remembered for my specialness like everyone else."

Feeling stung by those words I apologized. "I wasn't trying to cover you up or make them forget you."

"I know that. You just went along with it. What I'm saying is that it's time you and the family stopped that foolishness. If they won't, at least you can."

I felt like a heavy load had just fallen off my shoulders. Carrying Ed had made me tired and weary. I did not want to be him anymore. I almost shouted, "I am ready; boy, am I ready! What do you suggest?"

"You mean you don't know how to keep us separate?"

"Well, I could find out more about you . . . how we really were different. I realize now I know so little about you."

Pushing some more he asked, "Anything else you could do?"

"I guess I could tell the family that sometimes I feel like we are the same person to them." My thin voice and tense face told him that would not be easy.

"That is strong stuff, but I believe they will welcome it. I surely do."

The feelings that came next are hard to explain. It must be what a person feels after years of confinement, only to discover the doors to his cell are open, and he is free if he so chooses. Maybe it was fear of taking a step only to be told it was a trick or cruel joke. No, it was real, and I was free. If I chose to remain captive, I was my own jailer. No one else stood in my way to a new freedom. Finally, I hesitantly uttered, "I am embarrassed and ashamed. All this time I have been angry because I felt lost in you. Never once did I reflect or consider how you were being cheated, too. Now we both can be free. Thanks, Ed. Thanks for finding me so that I could find myself."

"Today has been long overdue; and, by the way, I *am* glad we look alike."

"Me too!"

"Let's go home and see if they can tell us apart."

Together we walked back to the house. I laughed inside and thought, "I not only found myself; I found Ed, and now for the first time I had a chance to get to know him."

A Conversation with Mary

"Oh, Mama B"

Is it my imagination or do grandmothers always seem to be in the kitchen? Mama B was not particularly fond of cooking but would always see that a good hearty meal was prepared. Somehow I felt if I were to chat with her, the kitchen would be the place. For some reason, I was always a little hesitant to reach out to her; so, I yelled from the safety of the living room. I take rejection better from a distance.

"Oh, Mama B, I need to talk with you."

With her gravelly but caring tone she called back, "Sure, Ben. Come on in the kitchen."

"Well," I mumbled, "I just realized we never have had a good talk. I don't know why, but I do have things to say . . . and there are some things I want to hear from you."

She slowed her scurrying around the kitchen and, believe it or not, sat down in one of the kitchen chairs. "Nothing would please me more. What is on your mind?"

With a gulp I said, "It's more from my heart. I want to thank you for those special days when I stayed with you in the summer. You really went all out to see that I had a

49

good time. You probably never knew it but some days I got so lonely that I hid behind a chair and cried. After I had been there awhile, you called me into this same kitchen and offered me a big bowl of ice cream. It was a great remedy for tears and loneliness."

"I never knew that . . . sure am glad I offered the ice cream. I would have done even more if you had asked or told me about your tears."

"Oh, I could never have done that then. I had to be a real man away from home, though I was only eight."

"I understand, but still . . ." She seemed hurt and I quickly moved on.

"Then, there was the time I went to see a scary movie. When I got back to your house, I was shaking inside. I was not about to let you know, but by bedtime I knew I didn't want to sleep in my room alone. You seemed to know and suggested maybe I should sleep in your room just that one evening. Boy, oh boy, was I glad for that. I didn't even have to admit just how scared I was."

She gave one of her deep, hearty laughs and said, "Your eyes told me that night, and I know what it is to be afraid. It's no fun for anyone."

That was not all. I needed to say more. "I just have to tell you about the time you and Papa took me to Myrtle Beach. You saw to it that I got to swim, play on the beach, and best of all, you even gave me money for the pinball machines. What a great time. You know, I didn't say thanks then. I don't know why, but it sure seems I held a lot back. Wonder why it is so difficult to say thanks?"

"I don't know, but I never told you how much joy you brought me." After a brief pause she continued, "I didn't do all those things just for you. It brightened my day. Your laughter and play reminded me of my boys. It was fun to relive earlier days through you. I was even able to do for you what I never did for my own sons. Maybe it was my way of trying to make up for what could not be earlier." Another pause and a deep sigh, "No, it was not a one-way street. I wished I could have seen you more. I never told you that either, did I?"

50

Feeling closer to Mama B than ever in my life, I quickly answered, "No, I guess we both held back. Oh, I don't know if I would have understood it then, but I do wish you had said it . . . just as I wish I had."

"One thing is for sure, Papa and I love you. Maybe instead of words we gave you gifts, summer trips, and bowls of ice cream."

I chimed in, "Well, none of it was wasted. Everything you did is a memory to treasure, and the ice cream . . . well it is still refreshing to this day. It will never really melt!"

I swear I believe she was crying and through her tears said, "I am so happy to hear that from you."

"I am happy that I have *finally* said it."

"Bless you, Ben."

"God bless you, Mama B, as you have me."

A Conversation with Dwight

"Hey, Dwight"

Dwight's favorite place was in or under an automobile. I knew after he got off work where to find him. He would always be in his makeshift garage, repairing his or someone else's car. Therefore, I found myself walking up his driveway late one afternoon. Familiar sounds came from the garage. I peeked in and called out, "Hey, Dwight, what are you doing?"

He yelled from under a beat-up stockcar, "Working on this crazy engine."

Bending down and looking under the car, I saw his greasy hands working away on parts of the car that I could never name. "How's it going?"

"Slow right now. I had a wreck the last time I ran this thing. A guy slammed right into me. Man, I thought I was gone."

I had been there. I remembered it well. My knees got weak thinking about it. "I know. I was there and saw it. Even Dad said he was afraid it might have killed you. Scared me too. I thought I had lost my hero."

"Hero?" he replied. "Me, your hero? Are you kidding?"

"No, I really mean it. I always wanted to be like you."

He seemed startled and asked, "Why in the world like me? I have never done anything."

"Never done anything? Your life sure seems exciting to me. You were always telling me about how fast your stock-cars and motorbikes were. Then there were the times you tried to outrun or trick the police. Man, that was exciting to me."

He didn't like that and said, "That was kind of foolish, you know."

"Oh, do I ever! It would have scared me to try any of those things, but it was fun living my adventures through you. You didn't seem afraid of anything."

Still not pleased, he quickly corrected me. "That's not true, you know. I was scared a lot, especially my last wreck. The doctor told me, 'No more racing.' I really thought that crash got me. I thought I was through . . . finished . . . washed out!"

"Hey, I know what it is to think you are a goner. Remember that day I nearly drowned at the lake? Talk about a 'sinking feeling.' I was only seven, but I will never forget it. You know, I always thought it was you who saved me . . . after all, you were my hero."

"Ah, that wasn't me; it was my daddy, your Uncle Lon. I never saved anybody."

I got angry when he said that and snapped back, "Now, that's not true. You saved me in lots of ways."

With a perplexed and frustrated look, he prodded me. "How did I do that?"

That was the right question, and I was happy to answer. "More than once you saved me from loneliness. You are more than a dozen years older, but you would always take time to play games with me, even take me to movies. Without you many of those days would have been dreary, but you 'saved' me."

A little embarrassed, he said, "That was nothing."

"Nothing? Maybe nothing to you but it was something to me. That's not all." I was wound up now. "You took my side when your daddy would play jokes on me. Sometimes he could be rougher than he realized. You knew it hurt and called him off. Man, I could have hugged you for that. Wish now I had. You even took my side once when my mom and I were having a go-at-it. I couldn't believe how you jumped in on my side. That felt so good."

"I don't even remember that."

"It doesn't matter . . . I sure do! Funny, I just thought of a story. It's about a one-room school in the mountains of Kentucky. The boys had run off two teachers and a new one arrived on the scene. A small but wise man, he told the students they would make their own rules. Being rough, they decided punishment would be given by licks with a razor strap. Lying was five licks, cheating five, and stealing ten. One day a little boy who was so thin his ribs showed through his skin was caught stealing a lunch. His hunger had gotten the best of him, and he took a risk. He got caught. Ten licks on his back would have been unbearable, but that was the rule. As the teacher started to administer the punishment, one of the big ruffians stood and said, 'Hey, can I take his place?' The class, moved by the unexpected but welcome request, agreed. The little boy watched as the older boy took ten heavy licks on his back and then walked back to his seat. Tears streamed down the cheeks of the little boy who had never had anyone stand for him like that. Dwight, I often felt like the little boy and more than once you stood in my place, taking up for me. Though you constantly put yourself in dangerous situations, I always felt safe and cared-for around you."

He seemed very moved and his eyes were misty. "I never knew that."

A deep sadness took hold of me as I said, "I never told you . . . Maybe if I had . . ."

53

I was sinking in my grief when he cajoled, "Hey, don't do that to yourself. I love you. We all leave a lot of things unsaid. I did." He was rescuing me again. "I am glad you are trying to catch up. Look, next time we get together I'll tell you some 'secrets' I have kept locked up. I certainly have my share."

I was already feeling better. My, how he could make me brighten up! "Sounds like fun to me. I know one thing. I am tired of holding back so much that I have to say to folks who mean so much to me. Today helped me realize that." After a rare, silent moment I told him, "You did it again. You lifted me up! See you later, and I look forward to those 'secrets.' "

"Count on it!"

IV
A New Beginning

A NEW BEGINNING

❖

As I reflect on the letters and conversations, many more faces begin to appear. I realize these are only the first of many letters I need to write, only the first awkward steps in initiating neglected conversations. However, the best part is that I have been reminded of those who are still alive . . . the hundreds of faces that I can see on almost any day and engage in conversation. These are the people whose responses I do not need to guess. With the dialing of a phone or a brief drive, I can hear them speak their own feelings. Better yet, they can hear mine.

As I discussed my book with others, I discovered that they, too, had letters they had never written. Many spoke of a desire to have a conversation that never took place. A common phrase was, "If I could have just seen him/her one more time." What I have experienced is the next best way to have that final talk or finish that unwritten letter. Therefore, for those who wish to write and converse as I have done, I make these following suggestions. First, select one person to whom you would like to write and begin the letter. As you do, others will begin to appear. Keep a pad at hand and list the names. This will allow you to proceed without becoming preoccupied with the new names and faces.

Second, plan your writing when you are not likely to be disturbed. Interruptions not only break your concentration, but also erase a mood that will be difficult, if not impossible, to recapture. You will discover distractions are intolerable during these private moments.

Third, write what comes to mind. Do not censor it and do not plan it. You can always throw it away, but give your heart free rein. The surprises will at times be painful, but overall the rewards and release will be worth it. If you try

57

to control what you are feeling and want to say, it will only mean you have things you will need to express later. Have not we all hidden long enough?

Fourth, one or two letters a day is all I could handle. It is an emotionally draining process. Do not rush or overload. Give yourself adequate time for each letter. Come back to it later if you need to. Pace yourself.

This book is a new beginning, one in which, out of the void and darkness of withdrawal, I share the light of my soul, my feelings. It is only a beginning. Already I have experienced inward resistance. Those old temptations to hold back, pay back, withdraw, and wait for others haunt me daily. These letters and conversations are consistent reminders of the high price of such emotional isolation. Risking is not a familiar pattern for me, especially where my feelings are concerned. I have, to my own detriment, been a master at camouflage. Thinking of opening up more, I find myself afraid of the pain of rejection and ridicule. Yet, I have learned that unless I am willing to risk experiencing the pain, I cannot experience the joy—the joy of a letter answered, a word returned, a special moment shared. I have lost too many of these. No more. Today is a new beginning.